Baroque Ornament

CD-ROM AND BOOK

JACQUES STELLA

DOVER PUBLICATIONS, INC.
Mineola, New York

The CD-ROM on the inside back cover contains all of the images shown in the book. There is no installation necessary. Just insert the CD into your computer and call the images into your favorite software (refer to the documentation with your software for further instructions). Each image has been scanned at 600 dpi and saved in six different formats—BMP, EPS, GIF, JPEG, PICT, and TIFF. The JPEG and GIF files—the most popular graphics file types used on the Web—are Internet-ready.

The "Images" folder on the CD contains a number of different folders. All of the TIFF images have been placed in one folder, as have all of the PICT, all of the EPS, etc. The images in each of these folders are identical except for file format. Every image has a unique file name in the following format: xxx.xxx. The first 3 or 4 characters of the file name, before the period, correspond to the number printed with the image in the book. The last 3 characters of the file name, after the period, refer to the file format. So, 001.TIF would be the first file in the TIFF folder.

For technical support, contact:
Telephone: 1 (617) 249-0245
Fax: 1 (617) 249-0245
Email: dover@artimaging.com
Internet:
http://www.artimaging.com/dover.html
The fastest way to receive technical support is via email or the Internet.

Bibliographical Note

Baroque Ornament CD-ROM and Book contains all of the images shown in the book *Baroque Ornament and Designs,* by Jacques Stella, originally published by Dover Publications, Inc., in 1987. This book was a selection of plates from *Divers Ornements d'Architecture, Recueillis et Dessegnes Apres l'Antique par M'. Stella, Peintre Ordinaire du Roy et Chevalier de Son Ordre de St. Michel,* originally published in Paris in 1658.

Dover Electronic Clip Art®

International Standard Book Number: 0-486-99580-1

Manufactured in the United States of America
Dover Publications, Inc., 31 East 2nd Street, Mineola, N.Y. 11501

001

002

003

004

005

006

1

007

008

009

010

011

012

2

013

014

015

016

017

018

019

020

3

021

022

023

024

025

026

027

028

029

030

031

032

5

033

034

035

036

037

038

039

040

041

042

043

044

045

046

047

048

049

050

051

052

053

9

054

055

056

057

058

059

060

061

062

063

064

065

066

067

068

069

070

071

13

072

073

074

075

076

077

078

079

080

081

082

083

084

085

086

087

088

089

090

091

092

093

094

095

096

097

098

099

100

101

102

103

23

104

105

106

107

108

109

110

111

112

113

114

115

116

117

118

119

120

121

122

123

124

125

126

127

128

129

130

131

132

133

134

135

136

137

138

139

140

141

142

143

144

145

146

33

147

148

149

150

151

34

152

153

154

155

156

157

158

159

160

161

162

163

164

165

166

167

168

169

170

171

172

173

174

175

176

177

178

179

180

181

182

183

184

185

186

187

188